<u>INDEX</u>

Doku Umarov

On March 29, 2010, two female suicide assailants blew themselves up at two separate locations along Moscow's underground network, killing at least 39 people. Two days later, the leader of the rebel movement in the Northern Caucasus, Doku Umarov, claimed responsibility for the attacks. For those monitoring the political situation in the Northern Caucasus, Umarov's claim of responsibility came as no surprise.

Even so, few analysts have been able to shed any meaningful light on Umarov's core political beliefs. This is not surprising considering that so much of Umarov's background remains shrouded in uncertainty.

He was born in the town of Kharsenoi in Chechnya's Shatoisky district in April 1964. Practically nothing is known about Umarov's childhood experiences. By Umarov's own account, his family were members of Chechnya's intelligentsia. The first substantial information relating to his formative experiences concerns his graduation from the construction faculty of the Oil Institute in Grozny, Chechnya's capital city, where he reportedly secured a degree in engineering.

Assuming that Umarov was approximately twenty-one years of age on graduating from the Oil Institute, this would suggest that his studies were completed in either 1984 or 1985. This was a difficult time for any young Chechen graduate to make a gainful, honest living.

Chechnya's economy became evermore dichotomised during the Brezhnev era. The republic's highly profitable oil industry, centred on Grozny and its surrounds, was dominated by ethnic Russians and the recruitment of Chechens and Ingush into this sector was actively discouraged. With job opportunities scarce in the republic's most lucrative economic sector, a majority of Chechens found themselves confined to their overpopulated home villages. The options facing this unwanted labour force were threefold: seek low-wage employment in Chechnya's agricultural sector; emigrate to another part of the USSR in search of seasonal, or permanent, work; or try to carve out a niche in Chechnya's shadow economy.

Not long after graduating, Umarov chose to emigrate and fetched up in central Russia. It is not certain whether the motivation behind this decision was economic or something altogether more untoward. According to certain sources, Umarov became involved in criminality during the early nineteen-eighties. One account holds that he was arrested in 1982 on charges of "hooliganism" and sentenced to three years imprisonment.

A second account details how Umarov was charged and convicted of "reckless homicide" in 1980, when he would have been just sixteen. While a third account claims that he was convicted of "manslaughter" in 1981. If we are to read anything into these accounts then Umarov must have spent a considerable amount of time in prison between the years 1980 and 1984 – in other words the approximate period during which he is supposed to have attended the Oil Institute in Grozny.

Regardless of whether he spent these years in college or in prison, Umarov certainly left Chechnya sometime in the mid-1980s. By the early 1990s he had established himself as a businessman in Siberia, in the city of Tyumen to be exact. Here, Umarov reportedly worked as the commercial director of the so-called Tyumen-Agda F4 enterprise. Umarov secured this job by virtue of certain family connections. The managing director of the company was another Chechen, one Musa Atayev, Umarov's cousin.

Sources close to Russia's security establishment claim that Umarov's time in Tyumen was cut short by a violent episode he became embroiled in during the summer of 1992. Following an altercation with a group of local teenagers, the exact details of which are unclear, Umarov and Atayev gained forcible entry to a house in the Patrushayevo district of Tyumen. The house belonged to a Mr. Alexander Subotin, whose son was one of the youths who had somehow aggravated the Chechen cousins.

Umarov and Atayev conducted themselves belligerently and demanded of Mr. Subotin that he turn over his son immediately. When Subotin asked for an explanation as to the two intruders' interest in his son, he was shot and left for dead (Subotin survived his wounds). The Chechen duo then allegedly executed a second family member, as well as a visitor to the household, before helping themselves to some of the Subotins' belongings and making good their escape.

By the time murder charges were brought against them in July 1992. Umarov and Atayev had returned to Chechnya, which by this time had declared its independence from the Russian Federation. Chechnya thus represented a safe haven for fugitives from Russian justice such as Umarov and Atayev.

Naturally, a degree of circumspection is required when dealing with source material furnished by Russia's military-security complex. It is possible that the Subotin affair, as well as the other accusations that have been made against Umarov, are parts of an "active measure" by Russia's Federal Security Service designed to discredit him. However, even one of Umarov's intimates, the Islamic theologian Sheikh Said Buryatsky, has acknowledged that Umarov was involved in racketeering during an earlier stage of his life.

War in Chechnya

Firstly, it should be pointed out that Umarov did not return to Chechnya "when war began". As we have established, Umarov returned to his homeland in the summer of 1992, almost two and a half years prior to the commencement of military hostilities between Dudayev's regime in Chechnya and the Russian state. Regardless of the correct chronology involved, it seems credible that Umarov would have presented himself to Gelayev as described by Buryatsky. This meeting may not have taken place until 1993, however, at which time Gelayev had returned to Chechnya from Abkhazia. The two men were related and it would have made sense for Umarov to waylay relatives in search of employment, just as he had done with Musa Atayev in Tyumen.

By mid-1992, Ruslan Gelayev was allied with Chechnya's nationalist leader, Dzhokhar Dudayev, a former General in the Soviet airforce. Following his election as president, Dudayev proceeded to declare Chechnya's independence from the Russian Federation. This decision ushered in a period of Cold War between Grozny and Moscow which lasted until December 1994 when Russian tanks finally moved into the rebellious republic as part of an attempt to "restore constitutional order".

Men like Gelayev, as well as the aforementioned Shamil Basayev, functioned as the military backbone of the Dudayev regime. Abetted by Russia's military and intelligence services, Gelayev and Basayev had fought against Georgian nationalist forces in Abkhazia in 1992–93. Basayev had come a long way from the aspiring student who spent the latter half of the 1980s peddling foreign computers and flirting with the world of organised crime. It was in Abkhazia, that he discovered a talent for war-making, as well as a certain flair for cruelty that would continue to manifest itself throughout his long career. Gelayev also found his niche in Abkhazia. In addition to honing his military talents, some reports suggest that Gelayev's involvement in the Georgian-Abkhaz conflict was notable for the cruelty he showed towards captured Georgian soldiers. Similar reports abound in relation to Basayev's treatment of Georgian prisoners of war.

Their exploits in Abkhazia bestowed a certain prestige on these two men. On returning to Chechnya they were feted as war heroes; Basayev's "Abkhaz Battalion", in particular, caught the public's imagination.33 Both Basayev and Gelayev positioned themselves as supporters of Dudayev and his nationalist agenda, although neither seemed to feel any great personal enthusiasm for the General. It was against this political backdrop that Doku Umarov appeared on Gelayev's doorstep seeking his relative's patronage.

One can readily speculate as to why Gelayev might have snubbed his plaintive kinsman so perfunctorily. For one thing, Gelayev had just returned from a particularly exacting, not to mention austere, period of existence on the battlefields of Abkhazia and may have taken umbrage at Umarov arriving at his home looking like a dilettante. Gelayev was also (re)discovering his Islamic faith at this stage of his life and would not have been impressed by Umarov's candid admission that he did not know how to perform certain basic religious rites.

The poor first impression he made on Gelayev was not to the detriment of Umarov's career in the long-term. The commander Umarov was directed to by Gelayev was Daud Akhmadov, an important figure within President Dudayev's notoriously corrupt inner circle. Akhmadov seems to have been the natural point of contact between Dudayev and Gelayev for he had the distinction of being on good terms with both men. This responsibility was more challenging than it might have seemed at first glance, for Gelayev and Dudayev were never on the greatest of terms. Indeed, in March 1994, scarcely eight months before the commencement of hostilities with Russia, Gelayev and Basayev were allegedly contemplating a coup d'état to unseat Dudayev.

As a member of Akhmadov's network Umarov's reputation began to flourish. By way of cementing his relationship with his new patron, Umarov married Akhmadov's daughter. His career prospered under wartime conditions and at some point during the hostilities he was drafted into Gelayev's paramilitary outfit. As a member of Gelayev's "Borz" battalion, Umarov would likely have participated in the defence of Bamut, a village in south-western Chechnya. Bamut became a symbol of resistance for the Chechen rebels and Gelayev would later be decorated with the "Order of Ichkeria" for his participation in these events. Many of the villagers hailed from the same clan as Umarov, the Mulkoi, and these bonds, as well as his membership of the Borz battalion, mean that it is likely that he participated in the defence of Bamut.

Umarov emerged from the war in a position of some political influence, with a military rank of "Brigadier-General", as well as two prestigious commendations for bravery in combat. In August 1996, the so-called Khasavyurt accords were signed between Russian and Chechen representatives giving Chechnya the status of a de facto independent state. In January 1997 presidential elections were held and Aslan Maskhadov, a well-known wartime field-commander, was returned as president, replacing Dudayev who had been killed during the war.

Sources indicate that Umarov left Gelayev's unit sometime between September 1996 and January 1997. It is unclear whether this decision was prompted by a falling out between the two men. Regardless, Umarov sought out and received the patronage of another paramilitary leader, Akhmed Zakayev. It may well have been Zakayev who recommended Umarov to Maskhadov as a candidate for the chairmanship of Chechnya's new Security Council. Maskhadov duly confirmed Umarov's growing political influence by appointing him to this post in June 1997.

Perhaps the most serious challenge facing Umarov in his new capacity as secretary of Chechnya's Security Council was the increased political and social instability engendered by the increasingly widespread practice of hostage-taking within the new state. In June 2008, Umarov explained the situation he found himself in as follows:

[...] we know that after the first war there was no unity among the Mujahideen like in the old days, and [that] the Mujahideen were organizing into groups. Since I had my group under my command, and since I had a military training base, it was impossible to remain outside politics back at that time, so even if you wanted to remain outside politics, they wouldn't let you do that, and the President of that time, Aslan Maskhadov, may Allah have mercy on him, appointed me Secretary of Security.

Paramilitary groups independent of government authority now emerged, as Umarov would later put it, "like mushrooms after rain". In hindsight, the calculations behind Maskhadov's appointment are easy to discern: Umarov was known to be on good terms with many of the major players in Chechnya's hostage-taking industry, among them Arbi Barayev, Balaudi Tekilov and the

Akhmadov brothers. Barayev, a field-commander of some renown during the first Russo-Chechen conflict, hailed from the same clan and geographical location as Umarov. It has since been claimed that Umarov used his new role as secretary of the Security Council as cover for entering into a freelance hostage-taking enterprise with Barayev, but this speculation has never been confirmed.

Umarov was also on good terms with Baludi Tekilov, an opportunistic former racketeer and pimp who emerged as one of the main point-men in Chechnya's hostage-taking industry during the late 1990s. Like Umarov, Tekilov returned to Chechnya in the early 1990s as a fugitive from Russian justice; he too sought to advance his political career through courtship, eventually marrying the sister of Salman Raduyev, a famous Chechen field-commander. Raduyev's resourceful new brother-in-law quickly caught his eye and he soon appointed Tekilov as his chief-of-staff. Tekilov used this influential position to carve out a niche for himself in Chechnya's thriving hostage-taking industry. Under Chechnya's post-war government, Tekilov was appointed head of the so-called Commission for the Liberation of Missing or Detained Persons.

Umarov has since claimed that it was his necessary association with the likes of Barayev, Tekilov and Akhmadov that led to him being accused of participation in the hostage-taking trade. In an interview with Andrei Babitsky in 2005, Umarov flatly denied any involvement in such activities:

Because of these contacts, I began to be accused of this [hostage-taking]. But I always – when these accusations reached this level, when Maskhadov said at the Security Council that I had been accused – I said, "Here is my statement, but a person's guilt can only be established in court. If I am guilty, I will not lift a finger to defend myself. Prove it and that's all. But what people say – that is slander, and it isn't for me. Just give me a fact. Without facts, a person can say, looking at a horse, "there is a goat".

Umarov is correct in stating that there is no concrete evidence of his direct involvement in the hostage-taking industry. However, in 2007, Umarov did little to enhance the case for his defence by posthumously honouring Barayev, a well-known hostage-taker, promoting him to the rank of "Brigadier-General". Indeed, this decision was especially strange given Barayev's known collaboration with Russia's intelligence agencies.56 Barayev had been stripped of this rank by President Maskhadov in July 1998 following a violent altercation in Gudermes, Chechnya's second largest city.

It is difficult to ascertain the extent to which Umarov was involved in Chechnya's inter-war hostage-taking business. It can be said with certainty, however, that from the end of the first war, Umarov was consorting openly with several known participants in the hostage trade. Barayev, for example, is described by Souleimanov as "the nation's most notorious ruffian and kidnapper". The Akhmadov brothers, meanwhile, were an influential presence in the Urus-Martan District of Chechnya during the inter-war years60 and must have been known to Umarov.

Umarov's association with such individuals does not, of course, prove his direct involvement in the hostage-taking industry. It should be noted, however, that one need not have personally kicked down doors and hauled innocent people off into captivity to have been an active participant in the hostage trade. Referencing a conversation he had with Alexander Mukomolov, a member of General Alexander Lebed's "peacemaking mission" to Chechnya, Valeri Tishkov, a leading Russian ethnologist, has explained how kidnappings were usually the work not of individuals but rather of loosely formed groups of field-commanders who would haggle with one another over their share of the ransom, sometimes even trading hostages with one another.

As secretary of the Security Council, therefore, Umarov need not have involved himself directly in the act of abducting ordinary Chechens, ethnic Russians, foreigners, journalists and other targets. Instead, he could have used this office as a means of offering protection and legal validation to associates who were involved precisely in these activities. Incidentally, these were the very grounds on which Maskhadov relieved Umarov of his official duties in mid-1998.

While the hostage-taking phenomenon represented the most immediate challenge to Umarov in his capacity as Security Council secretary, the refusal of so many field-commanders to recognize Maskhadov's lawful authority was another trend that demanded his attention. Many of these dissidents were war-heroes who had distinguished themselves during the conflict with the Russians. Most of them were receptive to the ideology of radical Islam and took a dim view of President Maskhadov's policies, above all his efforts to establish a normative relationship with Moscow. Well-known field-commanders like Basayev, Raduyev and Barayev openly presented themselves as paragons of Islamic virtue.

Barayev renamed his paramilitary unit the "Special Purpose Islamic Brigade". Regarded throughout Chechnya as a "Wahhabi", the colloquial designation for a follower of radical Islam, Barayev was collaborating closely with like-minded field-commanders such as Abdul-Malik Mezhidov, head of the so-called Sharia Guard movement. He was also known to enjoy the patronage of Zelimkhan Yandarbiyev, a leading figure among the radicals.

In July 1998, paramilitary forces belonging to Barayev and Mezhidov clashed in Gudermes with forces loyal to the Yamadayev family, the de facto custodians of the city. In his capacity as Security Council Chairman, Umarov was obliged to intercede in this conflict. Umarov would later describe his role in these events as that of a "referee", explaining that he had felt little enthusiasm for his official duties as Security Council chief. After a two-day-long melee that claimed scores of lives, Barayev and Mezhidov were forced to abandon their positions in Gudermes. Maskhadov announced that both Barayev's and Mezhidov's forces were to be disbanded and forbade members of these bodies from bearing arms.

This was a particularly difficult period for Maskhadov and his supporters. The events in Gudermes represented merely the latest in an increasingly long line of violent clashes between Wahhabi forces and government militiamen. Against this backdrop, and in the light of Umarov's close relationship with Barayev and other known Wahhabis, Maskhadov might have deemed it politically prudent to dismiss his Security Council secretary.

Apart from his compromising ties to Barayev, in any case Umarov had failed to stabilise the security situation throughout Chechnya during his tenure as Security Council chief. Therefore, while we cannot satisfactorily answer the question of whether Umarov abetted the worsening security situation by partaking in Chechnya's lucrative hostage-taking industry, we can conclude that he failed to fulfil his official mandate of providing a favourable security environment in the new state.

Scant information is available about Umarov's activities between mid-1998 and September 1999, when a fresh bout of military hostilities broke out between the Russian state and the regime in Grozny. This renewal of hostilities was precipitated by an ill-advised military adventure undertaken by Maskhadov's opponents in the radical Islamic camp. In August 1999, Shamil Basayev, in tandem with a well-known Arab Islamist, Khattab, led a large party of guerrillas across Chechnya's eastern border, occupying several villages in neighbouring Dagestan.

This localised occupation of Dagestani territory was received with hostility by many Dagestanis and militia groups were hurriedly assembled to assist federal forces in repelling the invaders from Chechnya.68 Although Buryatsky has claimed that Umarov took part in diversionary operations in Dagestan's Novolaksk District to cover Basayev's eventual retreat from the occupied villages, Umarov himself has made no mention of his participation in these events, nor have any other independent commentators.

If ordinary Russians were shaken by Basayev's operation in western Dagestan, they were outraged by a series of apartment house bombings in Russian cities during September 1999, which claimed the lives of over 200 people.70 Russia's security agencies were quick to uncover a "Chechen trail" behind these attacks, with the country's new Prime Minister, Vladimir Putin, promising instant results against the perpetrators. A new war between the Russian state and Chechnya now seemed inevitable. Maskhadov vainly attempted to establish a dialogue with his counterparts in Moscow, but Basayev's adventurism in Dagestan had made him appear weak, a president who was incapable of exercising control over those nominally under his remit.

The Russian administration showed no interest in negotiating with Maskhadov. With war now seemingly inevitable, the majority of Chechnya's disparate field-commanders resolved to put their many differences to one side in order to participate in counter-measures against the coming Russian invasion. In preparing for the Russian attack, Umarov resumed his collaboration with his kinsman, Ruslan Gelayev, aiding in the preparation of siege defenses in and around Grozny.

Although they still showed a willingness to collaborate on occasion, relations between Umarov and Gelayev were at best equivocal and would remain so until the latter's death in 2004. Gelayev had prospered politically in the inter-war period, receiving the posts of prime minister and later defense minister in Maskhadov's government. He also began to show a keen interest in Islam, garnishing his credentials in this field by performing the Hajj and by attending the World Muslim Congress in Pakistan in early 1998.

The Chechen defenders held their positions in Grozny until January 2000, when they were finally forced to begin an evacuation of the city. During their chaotic flight from Grozny that winter, the rebels sustained heavy casualties. Basayev's detachment blundered into a minefield, with Basayev himself stepping on a mine and losing a foot.Gelayev withdrew amid controversial circumstances, with Maskhadov angrily denouncing him for abandoning his positions in Grozny without explicit orders. Umarov retreated also, sustaining a serious head injury in the process (a bullet wound to the jaw-bone).

Umarov Death

Umarov was first reported killed in a statement on Dec. 18, 2013 by Ramzan Kadyrov, the President of the Chechen Republic. But one day later, a video showing the Islamic Caucasus Emirate leader was uploaded to YouTube.

In mid-January 2014, Kadyrov again claimed that Umarov is dead, and said intercepted communications between jihadist leaders in Kabardino-Balkaria and Dagestan mentioned the election of a new "emir."

Kavkaz Center tweeted that Ali Abu Muhammad, the "Caucasus Emirate's Sharia Judge," was "elected as new CE Emir by leaders of CE provinces." A video of Abu Muhammad was also released by the Islamic Caucasus Emirate on Kavkaz Center.

In 11-minute video clip was posted on YouTube showing the burial of self-proclaimed Caucasus Emirate head Doku Umarov. Two senior Chechen insurgency commanders, Khamzat (Aslan Byutukayev) and Makhran (Saidov), describe (in Chechen) how Umarov was poisoned in early August 2013 when sharing food with younger fighters, and died one month later. Chechen Republic head Ramzan Kadyrov promptly posted a screen grab from the footage on his Instagram account as definitive proof that Umarov is dead.

Byutukayev explained that Umarov consumed a small amount of food that younger fighters had obtained from an Ingush on the highway leading to Djeyrakh (in southern Ingushetia, bordering on the south-westernmost part of Chechnya. Four other fighters died of poisoning; Umarov survived for a month before succumbing, at dawn on September 7.

Makhran dismissed the possibility that the poisoning was the result of a deliberate attempt by either Russian President Vladimir Putin or Chechen Republic head Ramzan Kadyrov to kill Umarov. He said that, on the contrary, Umarov's death was purely fortuitous. Makhran disclosed that Umarov had summoned his senior commanders, and Makhran himself had arrived the evening before Umarov's death.

The video clip shows six fighters helping to place Umarov's body in the grave prepared for him and cover it over. The two other most senior commanders, Aslambek Vadalov and Tarkhan Gaziyev, are apparently not present. It was in the summer of 2013 that Gaziyev appealed to the Chechen Republic Ichkeria Shari'a Court in exile to rule on whether Umarov's proclamation in late 2007 of the Caucasus Emirate was justified under Shari'a law.

The first, unsubstantiated reports of Umarov's death had surfaced in January when an audio tape was posted on YouTube in which a speaker tentatively identified as Caucasus Emirate qadi (supreme religious authority) Abu Mukhammad (Aliaskhab Kebekov) related how he had learned of Umarov's death and that he had been proposed as his successor. The audio tape did not give any details of when or how Umarov died.

Kebekov formally confirmed in mid-March that Umarov was dead and he had been chosen to succeed him. But he did not divulge the date or circumstances of Umarov's death.

Emirat Kavkaz

In summer 2006, Doku Umarov became the head of the self-proclaimed Chechen Republic of Ichkeria (ChRI); it happened after the death of the previous President of the ChRI Abdul-Khalim Sadulayev, who declared, on February 13, 2006, his programme aimed at uniting Northern Caucasus into a single Islamic state. The grounds for declaring this state were found "in the unconditional duty of Moslems before the Allah to establish the rule of Allah - Shariat - in their controlled territories."

Already on October 7, 2007, Umarov, acting in compliance with this programme, abolished the ChRI and proclaimed a new formation - Imarat Kavkaz, having declared introduction of complete Shariat rule in *"all the territories of Northern Caucasus, which are zones of armed actions."* Doku Umarov proclaimed himself to be Amir of Caucasian militants, the leader of jihad and *"the unique legitimate authority in all the territories where mujahads are present."*

The Umarov's decree on declaration of Imarat provoked a split in power agencies of the ChRI. Ahmed Zakaev, former emissary of Chechen separatists, who is in London, and a number of deputies of the parliament of Ichkeria accused Umarov of self-withdrawal from his official duties and proclaimed transfer of the whole power to the parliament of Ichkeria. Ahmed Zakaev became acting prime minister in the government of Ichkeria.

The split between supporters of Zakaev and Umarov became still deeper this summer, after Zakaev launched direct contacts and negotiations with the authorities of Chechnya and ordered the head of the general staff of the armed forces of Ichkeria to stop attacking Chechen militiamen, except for self-defence cases. Supporters of the Imarat accused Zakaev of betraying Islam by recognizing the legitimacy of Ramzan Kadyrov's government and sentenced Ahmed Zakaev to death.

The verdict to Zakaev was signed by the Supreme Judge of Imarat Kavkaz Caucasus Anzor Astemirov, who is in search on charges of participation in the armed attack to Nalchik on October 13, 2005 and whom the authorities announced liquidated in the course of special operation in Nalchik on May 28. However, people from Zakaev's retinue believe that the death sentence was passed by one of militants' leaders Movladi Udugov.

In his interview to the Georgian information agency "Pirveli", Udugov named Zakaev's government "*a group of swindlers and speculators*" and noted that the ChRI could not have its own government, since it became a vilayat (administrative territory, - comment of the "Caucasian Knot") of the Imarat. Movladi Udugov added that militants' forces kept growing day after day, and 2009 became "the year of advance of the mujahads of Imarat Kavkaz"; he treated the declaration of Imarat as "the historically justified claim of Caucasian Moslems who had always used a slightest opportunity to get united on the basis of Islam."

Ahmed Zakaev's order to stop, since August 1, any attacks on employees of power agencies of Chechnya was not perceived by militants as a guide to action. The resistance of the armed underground not slackened, but even noticeably amplified. This conclusion can be made, in particular, after comparative analysis of the archive data of the "Caucasian Knot" and the open sources, which present statistics on the situation in Chechnya during equal time intervals before and after cancellation of the counterterrorist operation (CTO) regime.

"Kadyrov with Zakaev may agree for so long as they wish, but, basically, it'll give nothing, because separatists' armed formations are under control of Doku Umarov and under command not of the field commanders of the Ichkeria time, but of absolutely different people - 'Amirs of Jama'ats'. By and large, they see no special difference between Kadyrov and Zakaev," a leader of one of local NGOs gave this comment on the current situation in Chechnya to the "Caucasian Knot".

The activity of the armed underground is not limited to the territory of Chechnya - similar trends are also observed in the neighbouring Ingushetia and Dagestan, from where messages on crimes against militiamen and servicemen arrive in fact on the daily basis.

In April 2009 (the month when the CTO regime was lifted in Chechnya), Doku Umarov reported in his video address, which was promulgated by the websites supporting militants of Northern Caucasus, about revival of the battalion of suicide bombers named "Riyad as-Salikhiin". Then, he reconfirmed this information in his interview to the edition "Prague Watchdog" of July 4, having stated that "mujahads" were planning new "operations" and that for this purpose they had more opportunities than Shamil Basaev, who founded the

"Riyad as-Salikhiin" in autumn 2002 and then perished on July 10, 2006, in explosion of the truck full of explosive, which he accompanied to Ingushetia.

Soon after that, on May 15, 2009, a terror act was committed by a suicide bomber near the MIA building in Grozny. After that, the authorities of Chechnya made a decision to launch broad-scale special operations against militants with the aim of complete liquidation of the armed underground, which continue till now.

In the end of July, shortly before Zakaev's announcement of the above "armistice", one of the websites supporting militants placed a material that the field commander Moslem Gakaev had sent 20 shahids to the flatland Chechnya with instruction to commit suicidal terror acts against local law enforcers.

Soon after that, on July 26, militant Rustam Mukhadiev blew himself up at the theatrical-concert hall in Grozny killing several high-ranking MIA officers and two foreign citizens.

This incident was followed a whole series of self-explosions of suicide bombers. Thus, on August 21 in Grozny, two suicide bombers killed four militiamen and a local woman. The next self-suicidal action was committed by militants on August 25 in Mesker-Yurt village, Shali District. At night on August 28, two suicide bombers triggered their "shahid belts" in the city of Shali. Two more terror act were committed in Chechnya by suicide bombers in September and one more - on October 1. Explosions of suicide bombers were registered not only in Chechnya, but also in neighbouring Dagestan and Ingushetia.

In the morning on September 1, a terrorist-suicide bomber blew up his car near the northern post of the STSI (State Traffic Safety Inspectorate, also known in Russia as "GIBDD") in Makhachkala, where he was stopped for check of documents. 13 persons suffered, one of them died.

The most resonant, by the number of victims, was the terror act committed by a suicide bomber on August 17 in Ingushetia, as a result of which 25 persons were killed and over 260 others wounded. The investigation assumes involvement in this terror act of Said Buryatskiy (also known as Alexander Tikhomirov), the ideologist of militants of Northern Caucasus.

After the Imarat Kavkaz was announced as a religious state, Tikhomirov made a decision to join Doku Umarov's groupings, and in spring 2008 he appeared in the Sunzha District of Ingushetia, where militants had their bases at that moment. His sermons of radical Islam became well-known and, according to the YouTube statistics, rather popular. According to the "Novaya Gazeta", if Said Buryatskiy himself was the executor of the terror act in Ingushetia, each record of his sermons can become a most powerful ideological weapon, as many Moslems can follow him.

In his appeal of October 7, 2007, while proclaiming the Imarat Kavkaz, Doku Umarov noted that the struggle for the Shariat order should not be limited to the territory of Northern Caucasus, and even Russia, and called his supporters to global jihad.

"Today, in Afghanistan, Iraq, Somalia and Palestine our brothers are at war. All who have attacked Moslems, wherever they did it, are our enemies," said Umarov and enumerated America, England and Israel among such "enemies", and *"everyone who is at war on Islam and Moslems."*

In September 2008, a website covering the activities and structure of Imarat Kavkaz placed a message that *"at present, the armed forces of Imarat Kavkaz are essentially controlling the mountain regions of Dagestan, Ichkeria, Ingushetia, Kabarda, Balkaria and Karachai."* These territories were defined as *"the military activity zone of the armed forces of Imarat Kavkaz."* Also, *"the zone of subversive military actions"* was defined as the *"foothill and flat areas and settlements of the above vilayats, and also vilayats of Iriston (North Ossetia; on May 11, 2009, Iriston was abolished and included into vilayat Galgaiche (Ingushetia)) and the Nogai Steppe (Stavropol Territory), western and the Black Sea coastal areas of Northern Caucasus"*, and also *"the Pre-Volga and Ural regions of the Russian Federations."*

In September 2008, the resources, which support militants, disseminated Umarov's appeal to still more strengthen the struggle during the sacred Moslems' month of Ramadan, which was named "the best time for jihad."

The terror acts committed during several recent months by suicide bombers in Northern Caucasus lead to conclusion that the applied theory has passed into practice - in most cases suicide bombers blew themselves in crowded areas; therefore, not only militiamen but also peaceful residents became victims of these actions.

"*Those who are today at war in Chechnya and other republics of Northern Caucasus are no longer speaking about the struggle for independence of Ichkeria. They have absolutely other ideals and absolutely other goals. Umarov has transferred the war into religious opposition, where mujahads, that is, fighters for the faith, are on one side, and the other side includes kafirs (disbelievers), who had occupied the Moslem republics of the Caucasus, and their helpers - 'murtads' (turncoats) from among 'national-traitors'*," notes one of local observers in Chechnya.

The conflict inside the camp of militants in Northern Caucasus is now a dispute of two ideologies: of the *"separatist ethnic nationalism (the aim being a sovereign Chechnya even without the brotherly Vainakh Ingushetia)"* and the "universal religious project", where the fight of the individual is *"incorporated into the global jihad; and its final goal is not limited to Northern Caucasus, and even, by and large, to Russia"*, said Sergey Markedonov, deputy director of the Russian Institute for Political and Military Analysis.

In his opinion, the opponents of the authorities who fight for Imarat Kavkaz have a stronger ideological motivation than the separatists who were building the independent Chechnya on the basis of its opposition against the "empire".

"*It will be much more difficult to bribe or over-propagandize them (supporters of Imarat). The propaganda should be aimed not so much at them but at the doubting or hesitating population. And people hesitate for one simple reason - for absence of any positive policy of the authorities and, as a consequence, of positive social dynamics,*" Mr Markedonov wrote.

Shura Butrin, an observer of the "Russian Reporter", believes that ten years were enough to understand that Russia is unable to eradicate resistance in Northern Caucasus in the military manner. "*Doku Umarov proclaimed abolition of Ichkeria and creation of Imarat Kavkaz. Very few people paid attention to it, as it seemed that certain virtual matters were in play, just another name of a terrorist grouping. But it was a real point. Part of North-Caucasian population does not live in Russia. They would not like to have anything in common with it. For them, Russia is an occupant-state, which had seized their lands. There are tens of thousands of them. Naturally, the underground resistance will exist in this environment,*" Mr Butrin writes in his article "Ten Years of Second Chechen War."

The author emphasizes that within ten years the resistance of the armed underground in Chechnya has changed strongly: "*In the course of the first and second wars, they were scattered groups of people with very different motivations. There were heroes and bandits, peasants and occasional, ordinary people among them [...]. Most of them, when it became clear that the war was lost, joined Kadyrov. Now, the war is more invisible; it's easier to hide it - but it's much more serious. Resistance is now free of occasional people; it has turned into a religious sect with powerful ideology. Its basis is jihad. Militants have completely got rid of nationalist ideas; they are no longer interested in independence of Chechnya. Jihad is now their sense of life - their supreme self-realization.*"

Russian historian Boris Sokolov sees the end of struggle, held by Russian power agencies against Islamic rebels and underground fighters in Northern Caucasus, in one of three scenarios. "*Scenario No. 1: the Islamic underground is liquidated, and the national republics of Northern Caucasus remain in the Russian Federation. Scenario No. 2: the republics of Northern Caucasus get their political independence and Russia-friendly regimes set up there, capable to bridle radical Islamites. And, finally, scenario No. 3: an Islamic state - Imarat (Emirate) Kavkaz - extremely hostile to Russia - appears instead of North-Caucasian republics,*" Mr Sokolov writes in his article "What instead of 'Imarat Kavkaz'?" published in the "Russian Magazine".

"*By its multi-billion donations the federal centre buys the loyalty of North-Caucasian elites, while keeping eyes closed to the fact that most of the funds are plundered and used not to the purpose; so that ordinary citizens get just dribs and drabs from Moscow's gifts [...]. No wonder that mujahads with their adherence to the simplicity of primary Islam are highly popular among the local population,*" Boris Sokolov marks, adding that "Umarov's mujahads" coordinate their actions across the whole Northern Caucasus, irrespective of administrative borders, while the federal centre has to adhere to these borders in its policy.

Ruslan Kurbanov, another author of the "Russian Magazine", notes that "*salafization*" or "*fundamentalization*" of the regions in the Caucasus, where Islamic traditions were lost or undermined in the Soviet time (Nogai districts, Southern Dagestan and Kabarda), launched in early 2000s, has already become practically irreversible. He quotes Abdurashid Saidov, one of the witnesses of the rout of salafite communities of Dagestan: "*When the authorities started to combat the religious ideology with their habitual clumsy methods - by repressions and persecutions [...], a mass exodus of dissidents to Ichkeria began [...]. Persecutions have rallied fundamentalists, lifted their spirit, strengthened their will to victory and qualitatively improved their arms and fighting capacity."*

Meanwhile, the point of view of the authorities on the situation in the North-Caucasian region implies that the activity of militants here is not independent, but staged and fed from abroad, both with human resources (experts on subversive-explosion war and recruitment of new jihad adherents), and with materials means (money, weapons and ammunition).

"The Arabs who write fatwas for these actors: 'You kill a militiaman - and you're shahid at once,' are backed by special services, including American and English ones," says President of Ingushetia Yunus-Bek Evkurov.

As reported by the state body "Grozny-Inform Information Agency", founded by the Ministry of the Chechen Republic for National Policy, Press and Information, there are no official documents evidencing the involvement of separate leading world powers to the attempts of destabilizing the criminal and political situation in the North-Caucasian region, but the facts of the links of domestic Islamites with foreign sponsors are on hand.

President of Chechnya Ramzan Kadyrov is confident of possible liquidation of all militants and believes that to solve the problem of illegal armed formations, the efforts of law enforcement bodies of Dagestan, Chechnya and Ingushetia should be united.

In the territories of Chechnya and Ingushetia power agents continue their reinforced operations against members of the armed underground. The most significant results of these operations are the capture of Rustaman Makhauri, a mid-level militants' field commander and liquidation of a group of eight militants, headed by Abubakar Pashaev, Amir of Jama'at of Azamat-Yurt village, Shelkovskoy District of Chechnya.

At the same time, the deadline appointed by Kadyrov for eradication of the armed underground in the territory of Chechnya is permanently postponed. This May, he appointed the term of two weeks, in June - a month; and in September the head of Chechnya stated that 2009 is "the last year for bandits."

Kabarda-Balkaria

In recent years, the North Caucasus has experienced an upsurge of violence and terrorist acts. After the Beslan hostage crisis and its backlash on the Chechen movement's international legitimacy, there was a decrease in terrorist acts and indiscriminate violence between 2004 and 2008. Insurgency strategies in the North Caucasus changed after the establishment of the Caucasus Emirate (CE) in 2007.

After Moscow's announcement of the end of counterterrorist operations in Chechnya in 2009, the situation rapidly deteriorated, leading to an increase of suicide bombings and attacks against siloviki (power ministry) targets in Ingushetia, Dagestan, and Chechnya.

In 2010, while Ingushetia and Chechnya experienced a significant decrease in the number of violent incidents, the level of violence reached new levels in Kabardino-Balkaria and Dagestan.

An important change in insurgent ideology can partially explain the upsurge in violence and terrorist attacks across Russia. During the First Chechen War, the insurgents fought against the Russian state mainly for political and nationalist reasons.

The establishment of the CE crystallized and made official a radical religious trend among insurgents that existed since the end of the first Chechen war. In fact, we can identify four competing ideologies in the North Caucasus—a nationalist trend, as well as traditional, moderate, and radical forms of Islam. Our memo first presents a genealogy of CE and its new ideology. Then we describe these four different ideologies and assess how they interact and influence the religious and political situation in Kabardino-Balkaria. Finally, we focus on the main problems that should bead dressed to deal with the upsurge of violence in the republic.

During the Second Chechen War, insurgency leaders sought support from religious groups outside Chechnya to expand the insurgency across the North Caucasus. While cooperation started between jamaats (Islamic councils or assemblies) in Kabardino-Balkaria and the Chechen Republic of Ichkeria (ChRI), no formal structure existed. The idea of uniting all the anti-Russian separatist and religious groups in the Caucasus belonged to Anzor Astemirov, the leader of the Kabarda-Balkaria jamaat. In 2005, Astemirov and Ingush jamaat leader Ilyas Gorchkhanov approached Shamil Basaev with a suggestion to unite with the Chechen jamaat to form a Caucasus-wide coalition.

Basaev did not agree and suggested they subordinate themselves under the rule of the president of the ChRI, Abdul-Khalim Sadullayev. In exchange, Basaev helped insurgents in Kabardino-Balkaria organize a massive military attack on security forces in the regional capital of Nalchik in October 2005, which made Astemirov one of the most influential leaders in the Caucasus.

After the deaths of Basaev and Sadullayev in the summer of 2006, Astemirov proposed the creation of a Caucasian Emirate to Doku Umarov, the new president of the ChRI.* The new structure absorbed the ChRI and included it as one of its regions.

The CE was divided into six vilayats (administrative divisions). The new ideology was established at the foundation of the CE in October 2007. The establishment of the Emirate led to a clash between religious and nationalist branches inside the insurgency.

A group of insurgents denounced the transformation of ChRI into CE and elected a new president of ChRI, Ahmed Zakayev. This election did not prevent the creation of the CE. Umarov became Emir and Astemirov became Kadi (ideological and judicial leader) of the Supreme Sharia Court. The Emirate had two main goals: to change the ideology from separatism/nationalism to religious extremism and to establish an Islamic state in the North Caucasus— though they see themselves as fundamentalists and claim they are fighting for jihad (holy war) against terror perpetrated by the state.

During the summer of 2010, the ideological split among the insurgency leaders continued when Chechen warlords Hussein Gakaev and Aslanbek Vadalov withdrew their oath to the Emir but did not renounce their loyalty to the CE.

Many analysts and politicians claimed that the split was mainly a clash between nationalist and religious factions inside the CE. Others believed that the split was most likely about the leadership and power struggles within the movement. Recently, a change in the strategies of other vilayats could be observed. The Ingush jamaat announced its intention to stop targeting police officers to focus exclusively on nationalist issues, while the Kabarda-Balkaria-

Karachai (KBK) vilayat announced its intention to intensify its attacks and target not only siloviki structures but also "hypocrites, idolators, and necromancers."

We can identify four major ideological trends in the North Caucasus: a nationalist trend, as well as a traditional, a moderate, and a radical form of Islam. Without delving into the theological nuances, let us point out the main differences and antagonisms between these ideologies.

By radical Islam, we mean an ideology that suggests that the law and spirit of Islam should reach all spheres of society. This ideology is rather strict and judgmental of those who do not develop themselves according to the Five Pillars of Islam. The followers of radical Islam are not inherently extremist, but within this ideology they might develop what we call an insurgency ideology.

Such an insurgent ideology is characterized by terrorism and extremist behaviors such as the perception of security forces as a direct enemy, hostility towards Muslim leaders and scholars with differing beliefs and regarding them as "hypocrites" promoting anti-Islamic ideologies, and the exclusion of those who are not strict Muslims. The CE's first leaders had a common ideological ground and agreed with each other on terrorist measures against siloviki and moderate Islamic leaders who "betrayed" their religion by working with the state against the CE. As kadi of the CE, Astemirov was responsible for judgment against "traitorous Imams." Umarov organized actions against siloviki and "infidels."

However, they did not agree with respect to traditional Islam. The religious leaders of moderate Islam usually oppose radical Islam and regardits followers as heretics. They openly support and are supported by state authorities. Indeed, the latter regard the development of moderate Islam as one measure against Islamic radicalization and insurgent recruitment. As regional leaders publicly declare their support for moderate Islam and Imams, the insurgents react by labelling these moderates as "traitorous imams." Moderate Islam expands its number of followers to include all who identify themselves as Muslims whether or not they practice the Five Pillars of Islam.

In an interview, Anas Pshikhachev, the leader of the moderate Islamists in Kabardino-Balkaria, stated, "Everyone who acknowledges Allah, Koran, Sunna, and the Prophet is a Muslim even if he does not observe any practices".

By this interpretation, Islam is not a question of active faith but passive acknowledgment. The clash between insurgency ideology and moderate Islam culminated on December 2010 with the murder of Pshikhachev.

Another trend is represented by many local scholars and intellectuals who understand traditional Islam as an ideology of local traditions mixed with Islam.This ideology takes its historical roots in the strong moral codex of AdygeKhabze, which was established in the 18th century and based on the philosophy of Jabag Kazanoko.

The first debates between radical and traditional Muslims took place at the beginning of the 19th century. The prominent Circassian scholar Sultan Khan-Girei wrote in 1835 in his "Notes about Circassia" that Islamic laws were supposed to give preferences to local customs but that the new generation of religious leaders "often performs judgment by Islamic laws thus breaking the old customs."

Initially, CE leaders did not share a common opinion toward traditional Islam. Some advocated radical methods including violence against civilians, which proved effective in the past, while others supported a policy of targeted assassination against adherents to moderate Islam. The ideologist of the latter, Astemirov, could be seen more as a politician than a military commander. Indeed, the upsurge of violence in Kabardino-Balkaria coincided with his death in March 2010. Astemirov rejected the unnecessary use of violence against Muslim civilians; he sought the support of the local population and put forward a proselytizing strategy to convert moderate Muslims to radical Islam. Opposing such a policy, Umarov claimed that it was wrong to regard as the enemy only those who attacked insurgents directly.

In April 2010, Asker Jappuyev was appointed as the new leader of insurgents in Kabardino-Balkaria. The explosion of the Baksan hydroelectric power plant in July 2010, the murder of prominent Kabardian folklorist scholar Aslan Tsipinov in December 2010, attacks aiming to interfere with the local tourist industry in February 2011, and other terrorist acts against civilians have demonstrated the ideological turn among the insurgents in Kabardino-Balkaria. There was a disagreement among insurgents regarding the killing of Tsipinov, who was well known for his public activities and academic works in promoting ethnic values before Muslim ones. This is an indication that the insurgents have not yet overcome their internal disputes about the strategy to adopt against traditional Islam in Kabardino-Balkaria.

Those discussions came to the public's attention when one of the insurgents stated that many Muslims could not comprehend why they should have killed Tsipinov and how his death would benefit Islam. Tsipinov's murder took place right after the killing of Pshikhachev and was conducted in the same way. While Pshikhachev was executed as a "traitorous imam," Tsipinov was blamed for heading a group of "pagans and idolators," working to revive "ancient pagan festivals," and because he "openly and overtly opposed Islam and Muslims."

The fourth ideological trend in the North Caucasus is nationalist ideology. While in Chechnya and Dagestan, many insurgency leaders evolved from nationalism into radical Islam, in Kabardino-Balkaria these two trends almost never interact and even confront each other. None of the Kabardian nationalist leaders in the 1990s ever tried to present themselves as devoted Muslims.

On a larger scale, this can also be demonstrated by the fact that none of the thousands of Kabardian volunteers who participated in the Georgian-Abkhaz war were ever identified as supporting religious extremism or joining religious movements in Kabardino-Balkaria. At the same time, the Kabardian volunteers managed to form a political movement by establishing a non-governmental organization, the Union of Abkhaz Volunteers in Nalchik, with a rather nationalist program. Meanwhile most of the Chechen volunteers who participated in the Georgian-Abkhaz war are generally understood to have become Islamic extremists, including Shamil Basaev, their leader.

The gap between radical Islamic and nationalist ideology widened after the establishment of the CE, although its leaders did not have a common view on nationalism. While the main trend of the new CE ideology became anti-nationalist, Astemirov made several statements aiming to expand his supporters by reaching out to nationalists. On March 2009, he claimed that Sultan Sosnaliev, a Kabardian commander of the Abkhazian army during the Georgian-Abkhaz war and later a defense minister of Abkhazia, was on the side of the CE. The leader of the Union of Abkhaz Volunteers, Alexei Bekshokov, responded that Astemirov's statement was false and that the late Sosnaliev was never connected to religious extremists. In spite of the differences in ideologies, the insurgents in Kabardino-Balkaria never regarded nationalists as their targets.

The creation of the CE increased the coordination of insurgency groups in different regions of the North Caucasus and intensified discussions about ideology and terrorist methods. The insurgents' actions have expanded rapidly from the fight against the siloviki to targeting civilians for ideological motives. They are also getting more involved in the political and economic struggle between local politicians and business elites.

The new wave of terrorist attacks in Kabardino-Balkaria in the second half of 2010 and the beginning of 2011 demonstrated that the younger generation of insurgents has reconsidered their ideological positions. In the past, violence wasmainly targeted against security forces as insurgents avoided terrorist acts against civilians. Now, new insurgency leaders seem to follow a different ideological path by targeting civilians including ideologists such as Tsipinov and Pshikhachev, as well as orchestrating attacks against economic targets such as the Baksan hydroelectric power plant and Elbrus tourist infrastructure.

Arsen Kanokov, president of Kabardino-Balkaria, explained (without any specification) that the rise in terrorist activity could be attributed to the fact that some political groups were sponsoring insurgents to influence his reappointment. If the insurgency developed tactics of interfering with political events and even siding with political groups in Kabardino-Balkaria, it could mean that terrorist acts might increase during the upcoming national parliamentary (December 2011) and presidential (March 2012) elections.

Much depends on the position of state authorities in the near future. While officially supporting the ideologies of moderate and traditional Islam against radical Islam, the government continues to interfere with nationalist ideology, which could effectively take part in the battle to win the hearts and minds of the young people and limit the influence of radical Islam on them. Nationalist ideology in the North Caucasus has been emerging in the last two years in connection with the upcoming 2014 Sochi Olympics, which coincides with the 150th anniversary of the Circassian exile in 1864.

Neither the state nor the insurgents have paid much attention to the issue of the Circassian genocide, which took place in Sochi, the last capital of independent Circassia. State authorities denounce the very existence of the Circassian question, which makes followers of the nationalist ideology more passive in their support for state policies against the insurgency. Meanwhile, analysts warn that insurgents may use the Circassian genocide issue if it is not resolved before the Olympics.

In May 2011, federal forces killed several insurgents including the KBK vilayat leader. The choice of the new leader will probably have an immediate impact on the situation and on the insurgent's tactics. However, recent history also shows that it does not necessarily mean a decrease in the level of violence.

It seems Kabardino-Balkaria is now at an important crossroads. Violence in the republic might reach unprecedented levels this summer, as the season is usually more suitable for an upsurge of terrorist attacks. As we demonstrated, the insurgents have already expanded their guerrilla activities and their recruitment propaganda aimed at young people in the republic. In February 2011, insurgency leaders called for mobilization of all their forces in response to the announcement of the counter-terrorist operation in Kabardino-Balkaria. Uncontrolled repression of the followers of radical Islam by siloviki, as in 2005, might feed insurgency, ideology, and recruitment, furthering a spiral of violence.

Recent violent events against insurgents' relatives also reflect the growing tensions between insurgency and local populations. As an inadequate response to the terrorist actions, the Parliament of the KBR released a new initiative to place charges against insurgents' families. Also, an unknown group identifying themselves as an antiwahhabi militia named the "Black Hawks" has threatened (and committed) violence against insurgents' relatives.

Instead of putting forward repressive policies, state authorities should engage in various programs to promote political participation and social integration among young people. They also have to create a channel for political opposition that offers a non-violent alternative to voice political and religious grievances.

The case of Kabardino-Balkaria suggests that if no political solution is put forward to counter insurgents' propaganda and recruitment, further destabilization of the republic could result and insurgency ideology could spill over to relatively non-radicalized republics like Adygea and Karachaevo-Cherkessia.

The United Vilayat of Kabarda-Balkaria-Karachai also known as Vilayat KBK, is a militant Islamist Jihadist organization connected to numerous attacks against the local and federal security forces in the Russian republics of Kabardino-Balkaria and Karachay-Cherkessia in the North Caucasus. Vilayet KBK has been a member of the Caucasus Emirate group since 2007.

The group drew most of its early members from the Balkars, a small ethnic minority in the republic. However, their long-time leader between 2005 and 2010, Anzor Astemirov (Emir Sayfullah), was a Kabardin. Members come from other ethnic groups, including the Karachays and ethnic Russians. The group was named after the 7th-century Battle of Yarmouk.

The group began as a moderate non-violent organization named the Islamic Center in 1993. The group was renamed the Jamaat of Kabardino-Balkaria when it was not allowed to re-register under the original name in 1997. The focus of the group gradually changed because of persecution by Valery Kokov, the long-time ruler of the Republic of Kabardino-Balkaria, who labeled all alternatives to the local branch of the Spiritual Board of Russia's Muslims, operating the only official mosque in the republic, as Wahhabis, and indiscriminately and brutally harassed them.

Yarmuk was originally founded as a unit of around 30 Balkars and Kabardinians led by Muslim Atayev (Emir Sayfullah), which trained at the Chechen warlord Ruslan Gelayev's camp in Pankisi Gorge, Georgia. In 2002 the group helped Gelayev's forces in a raid of the village of Galashki in the Republic of Ingushetia. Upon their return to Kabardino-Balkaria, Atayev and his men launched a recruitment drive among alienated and radicalized youth.

Mounting pressure from a continued crackdown led the group's leader, Mussa Mukozhoyev (Musa Mukozhev), to join the underground. Many local young radicals had joined the Islamic Peacekeeping Army that invaded the republic of Dagestan from Chechnya in 1999 or fought on the Chechen separatist side in the Second Chechen War.

Radical Chechen commander Shamil Basayev maintained close ties with the local Salafis, living in the town of Baksan for more than a month in 2003, before narrowly escaping a police raid. An Ingush would-be suicide bomber, Zarema Muzhakhoyeva, lived in the republic's capital of Nalchik before going on a failed suicide mission to Moscow. A Nalchik resident housed the alleged organizer of the August 2004 bombing in the Moscow metro.

In August 2004 Yarmuk announced the beginning of military operations in the republic. Their online manifesto rejected terrorism, referring to alleged government responsibility for the 1999 Russian apartment bombings ("We are not fighting against women or children, like Russian invaders are doing in

Ichkeria. We are not blowing up sleeping people, like FSB of the Russian Federation does"). The manifesto noted the corruption of the "mafia clans" that led the republic ("These mere apologies for rulers, who sold themselves to the invaders, have made drug addiction, prostitution, poverty, crime, depravity, drunkenness and unemployment prosper in our Republic").

Yarmuk launched its first attack in Kabardino-Balkaria that same month, ambushing policemen in Chegem district. A turning point came in December 2004, when Yarmuk members conducted a raid on the office of the federal drug control agency in Nalchik, during which they seized large quantities of weapons and ammunition. The founding leader of Yarmuk, Muslim Atayev, was killed when the police stormed an apartment in Nalchik in January 2005. The organization continued to operate, staging attacks under the leadership of his successor, Rustam Bekanov. He was killed three months later and was replaced by Anzor Astemirov, a former deputy director of the Islamic Center. The group's base of operations was Nalchik and the Balkarian enclave around Mount Elbrus.

Yarmuk was the main force involved in the botched raid by around 100–200 mostly untrained militants on the capital Nalchik in 2005, during which more than 140 people, including 95 alleged insurgents, were killed. Scores of suspects were detained after the attack, and at least 52 were put on trial. The Jamaat apparently lost most of its members, including the deputy leader Ilyas Gorchkhanov. Survivors retrenched, and in late 2007 were subsumed into the United Vilayet of Kabarada, Balkaria and Karachay that would operate not only in Kabardino-Balkaria but also in the neighboring republic of Karachay–Cherkessia after the destruction of its native Karachay Jamaat.

The number of attacks attributed to Vilayet KBK at that time had been relatively low, being mostly targeted assassinations such as that of Anatoly Kyarov. One exception was the shooting of a group of nine Russian hunters in November 2007. The militants systematically kept recruiting new fighters and gathering weapons.

Following the killing of the groups leader Anzor Astemirov in March 2010, the leadership was assumed by more aggressive young commanders like the Baksan area-based Asker Dzhappuyev and the south-west sector commander Ratmir Shameyev, who regrouped Vilayet KBK and changed its tactics. The group went on to perpetrate two high-profile bombings: a blast at the Nalchik hippodrome that injured two ministers during May Day festivities and a sabotage attack on the Baksan hydroelectric power station that inflicted significant economic damage in July.

The group was also involved in a large number of near-daily attacks directed against members of security forces. According to a statement made by the Russian federal Interior Minister Rashid Nurgaliyev in November 2010, "the highest level of the terrorist threat in the North Caucasus is in the republics of Dagestan and Kabardino-Balkaria", as the KBR saw six times more gun attacks and nearly five times more explosions in 2010 as in the same period of 2009.

 The Vilayet KBK fighters began to simultaneously act as a Taliban-style morality police, targeting alleged "dens of vice". Between March and May 2011, the Russian Security Services killed nearly the entire leadership of the Vilayet, including overall Emir Asker Dzhappuyev, Emir Zakaria of the southwestern sector and Emir Abdul Jabbar of the Northeastern Sector.

The death of so many commanders led to a decline in the number of rebel attacks in Kabardino-Balkaria, mostly taking the form of attacks on local police officials and police stations. In September 2011 Alim Zankishiev (aka Emir Ubaidallah) became the new leader of the rebels, he was killed by Russian security forces in March 2012. A security operation in Nalchik in September 2012 again saw the killing of several senior commanders (Emir Hamza of the North-Western sector and acting leader of the group, Emir Abdal-Malik of the North-Eastern sector and Shamil Ulbashev, Emir of the Central Sector) in a single operation.

Ruslan Baryrbekov (also using the Nom de guerre Amir Khamza) briefly became leader before being killed in September 2012 when Khasanbi Fakov became emir. Fakov was killed by security forces in August 2013 in Nalchik, as was his successor Tengiz Guketlov in March 2014.

In August 2015, a video was released showing the leader of Vilayat KBK, Robert Zankishiev, pledging allegiance to the Islamic State of Iraq and the Levant (ISIL) leader Abu Bakr al-Baghdadi

Vilayat Dagestan

Vilayat Dagestan, formerly known as Shariat Jamaat, is an Islamist Jihadist group based in the Russian republic of Dagestan and is part of the Caucasus Emirate. The group, created during the Second Chechen War in favor of Dagestan's independence as an Islamic state, is responsible for the deaths of hundreds of Russian security and military personnel, officials, and civilians. The group is closely associated with the separatist conflicts in the nearby Russian republics of Chechnya and Ingushetia.

The Jamaat Shariat claims to be "*legitimate authority of Dagestan*" with the aim of establishing a "fair society" based on sharia law. To achieve this end, the Jamaat considers it legitimate to target police and security officials and some civilians such as the government-loyalist Muslim clergy and clerics of the Russian Orthodox Church. The Jamaat says that peace talks with Russia are hypothetically possible, but only when Russia withdraws its troops from the region and provides security guarantees. Otherwise, the group claims, it is prepared for a long-term guerrilla war of attrition that may be broadened to encompass the whole of the Russian Federation, including Moscow and St. Petersburg. As of 2010, the ongoing violence has plunged the multiethnic and corruption- and poverty-plagued republic into near civil war.

Shariat Jamaat was established by Emir Rasul (Rasul Makasharipov) following the near-destruction of the much smaller Dagestani terrorist group called Jennet. In 1999, Makasharipov fought against the government during the abortive rebel invasion of Dagestan from Chechnya. After moving to fight in Chechnya, he went back to his homeland in 2002 and set up Jennet (Dzhennet), whose principal objective was to eliminate senior officers of the security forces in Dagestan.

The group was loyal to the Chechen commander Shamil Basayev and its center of operations was the republic's capital of Makhachkala along with the nearby Tarki-Tau Mountain. The insurgents managed to assassinate several important figures such as Kamil Etinbekov, the Federal Security Service's territorial head of counterintelligence and counterterrorism; Akhberdilav Akilov, head of the police department for the struggle against extremism and criminal terrorism, and 28 officers of his department; and Magomed Gusayev, the minister of national policy, information, and external relations.

The 2002 Kaspiysk bombing, in which 43 soldiers and civilians were killed at a military parade, was also blamed on Makasharipov, although he rejected any responsibility and instead blamed the FSB director Nikolay Patrushev. The official Russian state media and its branches in Dagestan officially claimed that the bombing was organized by Rabbani-Khalil.

It was long after Rabbani-Khalil rejected responsibility and blamed instead head of Republic of Dagestan in one of his popular videos clarifying situation around him and militants in North Caucasus with historical pretext. Apparently the motives of the head of Republic of Dagestan was to discredit and blacken the image of Muslim militants that gained quite a popularity among the local population. However, there was no response to this claim of Rabbani-Khalil from the then head of Dagestan - Magomedali Magomedov.

Following the loss of several of its key leaders in late 2004, remnants of Jennet were re-organized and transformed into Sharia Jamaat (Arabic for "Islamic Law Community"). The new group, much larger and more decentralized (including the semi-autonomous local jamaats in Buinaksk, Gubden, Khasavyurt and Kaspiysk), is loosely organized mostly into many small clandestine urban cells, some with only three to five people, with a particularly strong presence in Makachkala.

The Jamaat also maintains several larger guerrilla subunits of up to 15 fighters each, which are based in the forested and mountainous areas of Dagestan and occasionally engage in relatively large battles against Russian special forces backed by artillery and air support (such as a battle in March 2009 in which 16 rebels and at least five Russian troops were killed).

The new group gradually became less discriminating in their attacks, targeting even rank-and-file traffic police officers, and killing more than 40 policemen in the first half year of 2005. In May 2005 it became part of the umbrella organization Caucasian Front established by the new president of the Chechen Republic of Ichkeria, Sheikh Abdul Halim, following the death of his predecessor Aslan Maskhadov. The group is believed to be responsible for many high-profile attacks such as the bombing which killed more than 10 Russian special forces soldiers in Makhachkala and the assassination of the republic's deputy Interior Minister, General Magomed Omarov in 2005.

Makasharipov was killed during a shootout with Russian troops on 6 July 2005, and his deputy Rabbani (Rappani Khalilov) then took over command. Rabbani was said to be an extremely popular with the youth and was able to recruit hundreds of fighters into Jamaat's ranks. He was closely allied with the Chechen rebels and the commander of foreign fighters in the Caucasus, Abu Hafs al-Urduni, and was killed in a house siege by the Russian special forces on 17 September 2007.

With the statements of the new Chechen separatist leader Dokka Umarov, published by Kavkaz Center on 1 October 2007, Khalilov was replaced by his deputy, Abdul Majid (Ilgas Malachiyev). Majid had begun his career during the Second Chechen War, fighting under Mashkadov and Ibn al-Khattab, before joining the Jamaat in 2005; this helped legitimize him as a rebel leader in Dagestan with the leaderships of both Chechen rebels and foreign fighters. Abdul Majid took the Jamaat oath to not attack civilians and was credited with bringing order to the group after the death of Khalilov.

On 8 September 2008, he was killed in a battle in southern Dagestan on the border with Azerbaijan in a joint operation of Russian and Azeri special forces. Following the death of Abu Majid, Umarov (now as the leader of the self-styled Caucasus Emirate) appointed Emir Muaz (Omar Sheikhulayev) to lead the renamed Vilayat of Dagestan. Emir Muaz was killed on 5 February 2009 in a gunfight with Russian special forces in a suburb of Makachkala.

He was replaced two months later by Emir Bara (Umalat Magomedov), who was in turn killed in a shootout at a police checkpoint in Makachkala on 31 December 2009. His place was then taken by Magomed Vagabov, whose leadership apparently resulted in the end to the ban on indiscriminate attacks against civilian targets. Vagabov was killed in a firefight when the federal forces surrounded him a house in the village of Gunib on 21 August 2010.

The continued upsurge of violence in Dagestan since 2008 included the killing of Gen. Valery Lipinsky, the first deputy head of the Internal Troops in the North Caucasus; the sniper assassination of Dagestan's Interior Minister, Gen. Adilgerei Magomedtagirov; and the massacre of four policemen and seven alleged prostitutes at a bathhouse in Makhachkala. In 2009, at least 58 police officers were killed in Dagestan.

The Vilayat Dagestan was responsible for a suicide attack on 6 January 2010 that killed six policemen; twin bombings in which two female bombers killed more than 40 people in the Moscow Metro in March 2010; and several suicide attacks against Russian security and military installations (such as the double bombing which killed 12 in Kizlyar). In February 2012, the Vilayat's then leader, Ibragimkhalil Daudov (aka Emir Salikh), was killed by Russian security forces.

In December 2014, the Vilayat's then commander, Rustam Asildarov, and a number of other members of the group publicly retracted their oath of allegiance to Caucasus Emirate leader Aliaskhab Kebekov, and pledged loyalty to Islamic State leader Abu Bakr al-Baghdadi. Kebekov condemned the defectors and appointed Said Kharakansky as the new leader of the group in Dagestan. Kharakansky and Kebekov's successor, Magomed Suleymanov, were killed by Russian security forces in clashes in August 201

Vilayat Noxçiyçö

The Province of Nokhchicho is the Chechen-based wing of the Caucasus Emirate organization. It was created in 2007 as one of the Emirate's six vilayats, replacing the Chechen Republic of Ichkeria.

The Chechen Republic of Ichkeria or CRI was an unrecognized secessionist government established in the Russian region of Chechnya in late 1991 by Dzhokhar Dudayev. After winning de facto independence in 1996 from the Russian Federation in the wake of the First Chechen War, it was invaded by Russia in the Second Chechen War, with direct rule of Chechnya being established in May 2000.

After losing territorial control to Russia, the CRI continued to exist in the form of an insurgent group fighting a guerrilla war against the Russian Military, while some Chechen separatists also carried out attacks against civilians in Russia. The CRI was severely weakened by the conflict with the Russians in the years following, suffering many casualties and defections including the deaths of its successive Presidents, Aslan Maskhadov and Abdul Halim Sadulayev. Following the death of Sadulayev in June 2006, Doku Umarov was elevated as the next leader of the CRI.

In August 2010, a video was posted on the rebel Kavkaz Center website showing Doku Umarov announcing his resignation as leader of the Caucasus Emirate and announcing Chechen commander Aslanbek Vadalov as his successor. This was followed by another video in the same month showing Umarov retracting the decision. Following these events, several commanders of the Chechen wing of the Caucasus Emirate - Tarkhan Gaziyev, Muhannad, Aslanbek Vadalov and Hussein Gakayev withdrew their oath of loyalty to Umarov. In a video, they also announced Gekayev has been elected the Emir of Chechnya.

In July 2011, a sharia court ruled in favour of Umarov and the dissident commanders reaffirmed the loyalty to him. Umarov then announced a reorganisation of the Vilayat into two military sectors, with Aslan Byutukayev being appointed as the head of the newly created Western Sector, and Hussein Gakayev being named as head the eastern sector.